Creatures of State

D0940821

Creatures
of
State

Brian Fawcett

Vancouver, Talonbooks, 1977

published with assistance from the Canada Council

Talonbooks
201 1019 East Cordova
Vancouver
British Columbia V6A 1M8
Canada

This book was typeset by Laura Lippert at Pulp Press,
designed by David Robinson and printed by Pulp Press
for Talonbooks.

Editor: Karl Siegler

First printing: October 1977

AWK: Sections of this book have appeared in: *The Capilano Review,*
Himma, Mayday, NMFG, West Coast Works, Yanagi and thru the
Caledonia Writing Series in Prince George, B.C.

Canadian Cataloguing in Publication Data

Fawcett, Brian, 1944-
    Creatures of state

    Poems.
    ISBN 0-88922-133-2 pa.

    I. Title.
PS8561.A92C74   C811'.5'4   C77-002213-8
PR9199.3.F

four documents
& a narrative
1974-1977

Cottonwood Canyon *a speech meant to be given to the Prince George Chamber of Commerce*

It begins with one 1957 International 180 refrigerator truck painted cream & white w/ Roses Ice Cream lettered big on the sides & across the front same & on each door Prince George, B.C.

        took the south approach to the Cottonwood Bridge 18 miles north of Quesnel took it too fast

  hooked the right front wheel over the guardrail & flipped on its side running the flat 90° curved approach topside asphalt & over the embankment into the ditch

        wheels spinning

         Stan Grayson crawls out, he's okay, scratches balding head w/ bloody finger & wipes same on the grey Palm Dairies uniform he wears

        saved for another job, mumbles

    sonofabitch

Leafy ditch, the river beyond wears patiently at the clay banks & overhanging alder & of course Cottonwood trees

        gnarled bark & wetroot uprooted by spring runoff from logged bush or bigcat lazy logging

   overturned in streambeds

        the great shallow roots exposed

Later behind the ice cream plant men stand around hands on hips

         it ain't bad, you can see the frame is twisted there but maybe we can use the box, only one side more or less buggered

        Names: Stan Grayson, Donnie Hanson, Bill Muldowan, Bobby MacAndrew, Alex Holobush drove same road

     new or same truck, eventually five trucks one V8 180 1961 good for 85 on the straightaway

        bragged to be the fastest truck in the north short of the bigrigs of Central Freightways or Ray Boris

         The others, including the 57 were 6's, 71 mph top speed at 2800 revs, nice trucks, pride of the road, pride of the men.

My story is about whether or not it is possible to take the south approach to the Cottonwood bridge at 60 mph & so make it up the north side of the river canyon without having to gear down all the way

                                        impossible

physically but necessary because men talked in the alley behind the plant & shrugged shoulders in such a way as to dispell experience & doubt

          tucking invoice books under muscled arms & walking off

                                            I don't

remember exactly their words, I was 16, 17, 18 standing around in the alley, then I was 21, doing the same run

                            finally doing the run & going

over the abstract problem of how to do it, abstract enough to try.

                                            I got

the truck to 45, the box leaning so crazily to the far side I wheeled & braked, disappointed

                 & not enough revs left to go more than ¼ mile up

the other side of the canyon before I dropped to 3rd under.

                                             What I

wanted was to make the long hill

                                wanted to be among these men I

recognized as congruent to the landscape drinking at the Stone Creek Hotel shitdrunk chasing the office secretary under the bridge to fuck around on their wives

                        at the company picnic at Nukko Lake w/ kids &

dresses as shapeless as their condition

                             which looked out thru their faces,

vague & dissatisfied as their men were, miles away & later, on the job, offering me advice about the ways of the world

                                  mostly shift down at

2750 shift up at 3250 & shift her smooth if you want to keep up yr revs punch the clutch & let her out of gear & punch her again & into gear or w/ twospeed just pop the gas & tap the red button she'll

                                        do all the rest if

you treat her right.

I wanted to think Great Thoughts & be sincere, change the world or die trying

          I wanted to treat them right & be treated right

                                 & to make the

south approach to the Cottonwood bridge at 60 mph.

The world from there was Hixon & north thru Stone Creek skirting the
Fraser thru Redrock & down the long straight past the airport, the
Giscome turnoff, Highway 16 east & down the steep twisting road into
the city, holding the empty truck to 3rd over

                                         & 4th under & back
again

       pumping brakes & shifting, empty reveries, emptied by the miles
& the thought of getting home

                              & getting in, getting the truck into the
plant, plugging in the freezer units

                              & driving up to Vanderhoof to catch
the drivers coming in from the west run standing on someone's
verandah, the west trucks half hidden by the trees, drink to get drunk

                                                or
just drink, fall down on the grass to watch the stars or someone with a
woman backed against a tree fifteen feet away hand planted in her
crotch, she moaning or just giggling, her father owns the Birch Drive
Inn or it's her squirreley married friend whose old man works in the
bush

       In the disintegration of Desire and the absense of Immortal Beauty
to puke into the grass

                        & sleep beneath the Cottonwoods.

II

At age 17 I was hauling beer up a set of backstairs behind Third Avenue
helping Bud Studer & his friend Eric who were bootlegging on the side,
some 25 or 30 cases a weekend stacked in the backseat of Bud's 56
Pontiac convertible I sometimes got to borrow. I was helping Bud but
not Eric who I wanted to go away & take his white socks with him, but he
goes into the bedroom as I'm stacking the beer in the kitchen, I catch
glimpses of a dark face & rumpled flesh, a dress, thru the doorway which
closes, waaap, Get the fuck in there Glenda. I want to say Hey Eric wash
yer socks I can smell yr goddamn feet thru the door & I want more to
Know Hey Bud who is that? Bud tells me it's nothing, uh, don't worry
about it, just some friend of Eric's staying for a week. Then a week later
it's my older brothers stag party & I'm there with my velvety antlers
drinking with four or five drivers in Bud's kitchen & Bud says why don't
we get Ron drunk & handcuff him to Glenda & put them on the train to
McBride which is such a famous local introduction to marriage everyone
says hah hah yah, lets get him so pissed he can't stand up & off we go
locking the bedroom door on Glenda who is indian & Bud is pimping,

or so Bob MacAndrew figures out & wants to sneak back later & screw
her before Bud dumps her, Bud explaining to me when I ask why he's
doing it, She's all fucked out & he was going to pour her full of cheap
wine & put her on the train anyway hah hah, get her out & Bob better
lay off cause she's probably got the clap by now & Bob is engaged to a
nurse & will I go head him off? I say sure Bud & I go tell Bob shit, man,
she's got the clap, you better cool it & Bob later pushes my unconscious
brother off the diving board at the municipal swimming pool we broke
into & then drove up & down the city streets holding up my brother for
all to see with puke running down his bare chest & his eyes rolling & by
Monday everyone is back at work & Glenda is gone, alone on the train,
to McBride.

III

The drivers had the emotional habit of living in one town & of looking
for love in another and of bridging the intervening distances with large
trucks & high speeds.
                    To turn thru the country of desire to amass velocity
& to carry their loads.
    Which is to say, ten years later, that they knew & cared nothing for
the country but rather took it as reflective to that which they drove like
hell to get thru in their own natures.
                            And driven by forces so close to my
own locked-in life I only now want to understand them as the totality of
landscape without undue emphasis on those interior mappings we
make so much of when there is apparently nowhere else to go except up
& down country roads.
                    Now that I know in both the weight of the
distances, the emptiness of the long road at 4 A.M. there is no romantic
confusion of motion & effect, nor of inside/outside
                                        or will you tell me
that the object of human desire is a shitkicking
                                in which the violence is
imagined?
            Okay, but you must explain the route of imagination.
                                                In the
lowlands it is the swift green growth of the cottonwoods, the soft white
wood feeding supple leaves that tremble at the slightest wind
                                                while here
among men & machines
                    is it Love? Money? Fighting & Killing?

Before
all these the cottonwoods fall, & the landscape is debris, stumps,
upturned roots
                    Yeah yeah, intoxication of blossoms, which I admit the
poets drink & sell on the cheap
                              but what of these other blossoms,
intoxications of barroom round table & beer to be knocked over or
thrown aside to get at someone sneering across a table
                                        or the intoxication
of new building & industry thick in the air & the music of bulldozers
                                                                  &
love-blossoms blueblack on the faces of women?

In the act of intoxication the interior roads lead away from the city we
might imagine
                    the landscape that might inform us & heal the wound of
the   dark   road
                         the   heavy   load   of   pungent   green   blossoms   of
cottonwood.
                    We need to know the purpose of goods delivered, whose
are they & what is their value.
                                   I accept the loving & fucking, the fighting
& killing
          but in the heart of the landscape where darkness gathers there
are no answers
                    & the questions get caught in the shifting of transmission
gears.

                                        IV

A driver named Bill Reese once busted up six soldiers from the USAF
radar base—ambushed them in the alley & put four of them in the
hospital because they called him a yokel in the Canada Hotel bar & he,
5/8 & 155 lbs said nothing but stared back for a moment then quietly
went outside, picked a length of 2x4 & found the olivegrey military
travelall, lifted the hood, tore out the distributor cap & squatted in the
darkness of the alley.

Just as he waited another time outside the hospital for Tim LaChance
after Timmie suffered an insulin convulsion drinking in the Simon
Fraser fell over onto the table knocking the beer flying, the others saying
what the fuck is this & going home to change clothes or to sleep it off.

                                                                  11

Bill quit without warning & disappeared much as the others
disappeared, only to show up the next spring looking for a job & sure to
get it because he could drive 360 gravel miles to Hazelton throw off his
load and be back 18 hours later ready to go next morning at 7 &
muttering because his truck isn't loaded

dark face vaguely dirty across
bridge of thin nose big pores & eyes small & cagey like a big
weasel

wolverine crossing swampy meadow to cabin, pushes open the
door scraping heavy fur on the jamb before shifting inside

& other
animals

just animals, Alice Bluegarden dragging herself out of the
creekbed with come on the front of her red & navy print dress & a look
on her face that revealed irrevocably to anyone who cared to see it that it
is possible

to shitkick the human soul.

So the descent again into Cottonwood Canyon & the attempt to alter
the centre of gravity of GVW 24000 lbs, 12 tons of metal & ice cream
hurtling into the abstract

& skidding on the bullshit laid down between
men

while bright water flowed beneath the bridge & fluttery poplar
leaves twisted & fell year after year until eternity takes away all the
names & faces & the trucks scrapped in some junkyard paint peeling,
decomposing under mounds of leaves & poisonous metals.

V

Just desserts, someone says, just desserts.

As if the orders were known,
justice properly distributed & the heart able to shake off the absence of
possessed & possessing landscape & follow the body to live on the
coast.

It isn't so. Property is not understood, & is distributed by
violence. Just desserts?

Just deserts

of balding men selling Uniroyal tires
deserting one town for another for a better paying job "great" future,
children growing up, to do the same?

& the women, they tire too,

continuity a knot of cancer in the uterus (removed). They say
even the
V8s tire out, con-rods wobble & then punch thru, or bearings seize &
the camshaft

O my pretty trucks all old & battered & the drivers unable to do hard
labour sell tires or bearings or milkshake cups & get shitkicked at the
Smithers Hotel by younger men in new trucks running out to Hazelton
up paved roads at 3500 revs, dumb young punks w/ more muscle than
knowhow, grabbing the waitresses by the ass & howling
whooobaby
why
don't we roll on back to Telkwa
booom
& drink all night in my hotel
room
& she smiles & off they go
vrrooom

Photograph these men. They stand in a group, so, several of them
slouched against the stucco wall, others performing vague aggressions
for the camera, hands on hips, lighting cigarettes, looking thru their
steelcovered invoice books. I'm there, in the corner, looking for
something to sit down on.
Film them. Film them driving or fighting or
making love. Film them delivering useless goods. Film them asleep with
their faces emptied of will & of explanation. Film them talking to one
another, shuffling their feet back against whatever draws them into the
desire to push the others away.
Imagine them with antlers. Imagine
them with claws & teeth. Imagine them with what they have. Imagine
mile upon mile of dark trees thru which rivers run. Imagine trucks, fast
cars, mile upon mile of highway. Imagine Cottonwood Canyon.

VI

The year I left the city Jack Duncan quit & I hired on after a three year
absence as the supervisor. The pulpmills were going up on the riverflats
to the northeast of the city & drivers came & left, as Jack said before he
quit, like flies on the asshole of a deer, brushed off by the hard work or
simply drifting away to easier pickings. Bill Reese was back again, Bill
Muldowan left his wife & kids & went to work in Edmonton, Bobby

MacAndrew quit to run his parent's store, Stan Grayson went east. Bud Studer was in Vancouver working a door-to-door bleach business & living with an indian woman with six kids. Tim LaChance was on the truck that serviced the vendors in & around town, a nice crazy kid of 18 everyone told me to keep an eye on, & I hired on Danny Gale to do the city truck run out east & north on Wednesdays & Fridays. I did the runs to Fort St. James & Endako, long 16 hour days I used to train new drivers, picked them up at the Unemployment Office at 7 A.M. & tried to break their backs running six cases of Pepsi-Cola at a time down the stairs of the Fort Cafe. If they could stay on their feet all day I kept them on—someone was always quitting, big money all over town & my father about to sell out under pressure from the big companies from the coast threatening to come in anyway & drop the ass out of the market by dumping below cost. They big enough to take 5 years of losses & my father, hypnotized by the rustle of money & slick coast lawyers offering him deals.

In the foreground of this landscape are the tall groves of cottonwood trees, yellowgreen, cottontipped in May

                                               transcient as the trucks I park beneath them.
                       And the background, abstract & hindsought

                                                    is the gutting of a city, the dismissal of its dreams into actuality.
    Prince George is the manifestation of the collective dream of its citizens

                a dream of wealth, progress, sophisticated industry pouring goods to world markets

                        the dream of a generation of men during the 1960's at the beginning of old age,

                                who came to the city in the 30's and 40's to escape the hungers of the big cities & came with a fierceness to work & make money

                    women to raise children

                                my mother at age 35 walking downtown along wooden sidewalks in a white dress, the streets crowded with indians in town for a murder trial

                                This, she said, is a safe place to raise my children.
                          & my father to build a house, white paint & the planting of crabapple, elm & mountain ash

                                These men grew old rushing at the shimmer of dollars

shafting their friends
some of them
hatchetmen for Netherlands Overseas or Northwood Pump & Paper
overbidding timber licences to knock off small mills
They dreamed at
night of paper money
in banks made of plywood
& they believed it was
just & progressive when the pulp mills came to push them out
forced
retirements in warmer climates or dying in basement recreation rooms.

They were victims of their own golden rule
If you
have a friend
who is fair
& true
        fuck him
                before
                        he fucks you.

The city empty, Third Avenue cluttered with refuse, the remnants of
the downtown businessmen building parkades & a freeway system,
forgetting the most simple truths of the landscape, that if you divert the
flow of a creek, logging debris chokes the old channel & backs up, as
simple to see as the truth that money moves with greatest force where it
has mass & an absence of moral constriction
& further on, that it collects
garbage & kills the trout before it kills the junkfish, attacks the hearts &
lungs, winter fog & stink from the mills & the homes of dead
lumbermen on Taylor Drive inhabited by lawyers & managers
Just
desserts
        Or deserts of rootless people serving the invisible keepers of
this paradisal garden, grown for what values?
Birch & alder for
firewood, the rest for pulp, saskatoon & huckleberries for bears & bears
to shoot, trucks for ice cream, useless & creamy, red & cream trucks
the congruous blossoms of this constructed garden
In the roar of the
motors, money, money talking, a bedlam of opportunity, opportunity
drowning the cries of confusion & pain in a undertow of booze & the
rivers full of dead cottonwoods & sewage & sulphur from the mills into

which at blinding speed

                         who turns the corner of two weeks holidays a
year & the threat of eternity

                            at 25 mph like the sign says, shifting down
to 4th under & a quick look at the water under the steel girders of the
bridge.

VII

The road west out of Prince George runs to the crest of a hill overlooking
the farmland of Mud River Valley

                      looks out over miles of troubled sky,
hills, lakes & rivers without end dominated by forests running from
watery black spruce to balsam & white spruce to fir & lodgepole pine as
it ascends to paradise which the roads cut off leading down & over thru
gravel & hardpan

                into the easy rolling country of Vanderhoof

                                  & Fraser
Lake, Fort Fraser, Francois Lake, Endako, Burns Lake. The truck rolling
in behind the New Omenica Cafe for lunch or gassing up at Three
Gables Service

            & what do any of these names mean, memory of trucks,
motors, & vistas of landscape thru bugspeckled windshield,

                               reluctant
love of this land which turned me out geographically & otherwise thru
Cottonwood Canyon to the coast

                    My land of "retired" forefathers,
logged off hillsides polluting creeks & rivers that run too fast & uproot
the cottonwoods just as we are uprooted

                    cut off from the knowledge of
place.
     We can do nothing but wander the streets or speed down
highways in machines we barely understand

                       while wraiths of the
knowledge look to make a fast buck & head for the coast

                          or are drunk
under the porches in the moonlight

               & beneath the green lawns & houses
of the dream nightmares grow visible like shit boiling from abandoned
cesspools

         & the children of the dream search foreign libraries & the
children's children grow up in daycare centres at the expense of the

government in cities too large for place & names.

This landscape moves
and changes with the seasons
from heat to cold
from snow to fire
& there
is no such thing in nature as
retirement
there is only death & life
& the
effort to make things clear to ourselves

& to make that clearing visible
& outside Vanderhoof heading west Bill
Reese & Tim LaChance in a borrowed 2 year old Chevy V8
Bill turns to
Tim, says crack me another beer, we'll make Smithers before the bar
closes, Tim's pockets full of stolen quarters from the machines, simply a
matter of faking the loadsheets to make the PepsiCola he puts in the
machines cease to exist for the company & to put heavy dollars in his
pockets to ease the ceaseless hours of life between insulin injections or
the next attempt to tear apart some deserving town to the west.

VIII

Bill & Tim's work is finished, their trucks are empty, parked in the alley
behind the plant. Bill & Tim pick up another dozen beer in Burns &
drink it. Watch them go, 80, 85, 90, Telkwa.
The road is like the back of
Bill's hands, known, knotted, scarred by his doings, 95, 100
The lights
of the car point ahead, down a little, & ahead into the valley of the
Bulkley River, 105
until the road suddenly is not ahead, it isn't there,
no,
there is the switchback, 110
and before Bill Reese is the forest, the 30
inch diameter of a Cottonwood ten feet & a split second away &
then
there is nothing at all except Bill's intestines drooping over the
crushed steering wheel & twisted metal & glass of the car & blood

17

spreading onto the seat & 50 feet away Tim's brains cooling on the trunk of another cottonwood in the night air gemmed with glass from the windshield & the moonlight & the car beginning to burn, small flames licking the hair from Bill's torn legs

until years later I come here to challenge what seem the true events of the years

the destructiveness of these interior roads cut thru cottonwood & undercut by rivers

to overturn

in your hearts the roots of this dream

comes to a blood red flower

the heart of it

burned black

& I ask you to look & I demand

that we act.

Will we turn

& uproot or will we burn the land?

The Fall of Saigon

This morning spring storms, the sky
grey & the earth blossom white
outside the window, white cherry blossoms
flaking off & falling
into the garden
                    I'm filled
with anxiety, I want
to surrender
to the possible, I'm tired
of what is given me
to do, these stolen tales
brought in like the cherry boughs
from the cold

                    Old Eros & mother Nature
are passive now to both theft
& oil spills
                    & the trespassing stories
perceived by the body & told
in the heart
don't hold
where the present order maintains its dreamless sleep

The form of the truth
is not to be found there
                              or if
in quantities that make no difference
to the conditions even so close as
the next yard
where the cherry tree roots
& rots with inattention, overhangs
my yard
          property

When the news came over the car radio telling us that Saigon had
unconditionally surrendered to the Viet Cong in order, it said, to avoid
bloodshed & that the troops had entered the city unopposed
                                                                                    I was
driving with friends along a dirt road toward the Cowichan Indian
Reserve on Vancouver Island. Our intention was to look at an old church

built of stone on a high hill well above the dying maples of the valley,
but the road was blockaded by a bunch of indian kids who stopped the
car and crowded around demanding money if we were to get thru,
demanding 50c to see the duck they had, which turned out to be a joke
when we paid it, a badly-done engraving of a duck quickly pushed thru
the window of the car and quickly pulled back, & did we want for a
dollar to see The Flower one of them held behind her back, paper
mache.

      While the news report was repeated & we drove on, the kids
having succeeded in getting a mutually acceptable toll, the stone church
in the distance

              But on the other side we were driving a captured
american tank into Saigon waving russian rifles, there were people
waving back, mostly happy, some were just relieved & some were
frightened but a city had surrendered

                        it had been proven

beyond all doubt

that neocolonial wars could no longer be won
& human history would be forced
to alter its course
              to surrender to new forces
the stone church built at the top of a hill
to overlook the reserve
             built 1870
& reconstructed 1966 to demonstrate the
powers of Heaven & Earth
               financed by the selling
of butter made by the priest & sold to the local whites
to provide money for materials & skilled labor
                      this house
in which to house the innocence of souls
                   & tame the
passions of the body,
          (later the government

The kids play
ballhockey on the new concrete floor,
or sit in the empty window frames
(the stained glass removed to Saltspring)

looking out over the bay & waiting
for the rain to stop
                    The first order
of the provisional revolutionary government
was to stop prostitution & to close dancehalls
in order to begin breaking down
the personal skills of exploiting human needs
& of accumulating property & power over others
& to begin the re-education
of teachers

And I am possessed
by anxiety here
where there is so little to surrender
the blossoms I brought into the house days ago
will wither, Old Eros
                    Dame Nature
                                    the sole property
of the body
is Time
which I am tired of squandering
on amusements & of selling it
as labor for useless tasks

                    for the intelligence
there is a vast field not to possess
but to reconstruct
                    after the surrender
there are the defoliated landscapes in which
herbicides must be broken down
that food may be grown again
                                    for the intelligence
to surrender to this reconstruction
                                    & the
displacement of economic forces so that
the wealthy no longer fly over the cities in
half-empty planes at public expense
while the poor beneath them
die in overcrowded hospital corridors
while experts talk of the need for
maintaining present technological priorities
due to world market pressures & the need

for jobs & the upkeep of national dignity
& the functionaries trade the commonwealth for
their own advancement & protection
& the unions trade money & time with the bosses
& say nothing about knowledge of
or control over
the means of production

                              Our polity
is greed & violence
puffed by the personal
                         & it seeds on the wind
like the dandelions on the roadside
                                   which
if you press down & cover with plastic
the leaves grow less bitter & the roots
sweeten, can be eaten
                      or is that like the way
the western press talked of
the strategic withdrawal of the
South Vietnamese Army
                         Until the surrender
& the Viet Cong forces entered the city
it was impossible to tell
that the South Vietnamese armies were
compelled by another force
                         are the forces
that defeated America in South East Asia
so invisible
          that American intelligence
could actually believe that the end of the Vietnam War
was a withdrawal?
                    Now the newsmen
talk of isolation, *New Isolationism*
puffs out into public language
& the nation swells again with
purity & self-importance—

                    Like hell,
America is collapsing, it is simply being defeated
without intelligent understanding of the causes,
ferrying its finks & victims in barges

to camps at Guam & Manila, thence via 747
to the mainland, absorbing them
into the body politic, into the disarray
of economic & sexual deception
that created the Vietnam War
                              while that
nation diverts itself of the image of defeat
Nixon hobbles along pacific coast beaches
on legs bloated with disease
the blood doesn't run anymore, clots
choke the flow as it returns
                              Mekong River
blocked by barges sunk by Viet Cong mortars
until the government begins to choke on its
own supplies

                    Nixon
looks out from the heart of America
we are all subject to, he
is still the image of its activity
                              for which
there is no imaginable pardon
                              only surrender
& not simply surrender before violent force
                              in the dark
the stone church beyond the maples of Cowichan Valley
is empty but beneath the maples
the children surrender to sleep, the men
& women surrender to the other
                              bearing the arms
of dreams & the world
                    & in Saigon
soldiers sleep in the doorways of paradise
& the stench of gunpowder & gasoline
surrenders in the streets
                         & our own streets
clear for a moment
                    hold a possibility of more
than the possession
of stolen blossoms

Elegy Written by the Shores of an Okanagan Lake   *after Thomas Gray*

Aircraft in flight, the 8:00 P.M.
via Cranbrook to the coast
low tooop of bullfrogs
in a far bay, carp splash
in the weedy shallows
                              & cars pass
between the bench & the road
                              none of it
belongs to me or to the darkness
                              which spreads
from both the north & south
because moon rise trails & hesitates
along the broken rim of eastern hills
                              as I

hesitate

We feel alone we
don't want to own any of it.

It isn't that words fail me
or that ancient motions of the moon & stars
cease to delight but

above me in the abandoned orchards
apricots rot
            & next to the armoured seed
bloated hornets sleep

                  Earlier in the day
there was the problem of
reaching into the trees to pick
& not step on the feeding hornets
or to be frightened to violence
by a bullsnake slipped thru the grass

The orchard is private property,
is fenced against campertrucks
or thieves like me
most trees dead & they want

to cut them all down
to keep spraying costs in line
for the managed orchards to the north
& all I am asked is

does the Old Moon Abide, is it full
of loathing?
Such concern for the sylvan hey
the farmers still work, they sell peaches
in styrofoam cartons to the tourists
& space in the orchards for campers
& the people eat peaches
play cards in the backs of the trucks. Yeah

the heavenly bodies still play
divine games, spread their designs
over the surface of the lake the wind
comes up, pushes the new weed

onto the subdivided shore, but

we must also know & say that
capitalism succeeded on this continent
because of the possibility of expanding
into contiguous markets & landscapes

& we have come to the end here
in the particular instances
Penticton, Princeton, Prince George

that ability to expand cut off
by the pacific ocean
& by more energetic peoples
in the hungry third world

& the contraction
in the value of our capital (& our Eros
reveals the interior destructions
the landscape ripped & convulsed
empty of material & cultural accretions
which might possibly be
an alternative to what we experience
in political & economic reality

as progress.

At the supermarket
the fruit is from California
but from there no place
there is no place to go
& the moon doesn't want us.

This elegy is occasioned by
no single death but now we all can see
beyond subsistence & stand
on the far bank of the
frozen current of the soul. let
some Glory & Grandeur rip this mortality
& Memory reopen the knarled & cankered
wounds of experience

& mock our useless toil
until this orchard landscape
& pleasured lake is burnished
by the generated heat
to mirror the boughs of blackened apricot

Let it burn
until the quiet of ashes
breeds new trees
and bees supplant
the carrion hornets.

And me? No, I
will go away, will not mark
the pleasures of these shores,
will forgo the clear heavens,
will pass the shattered orchards
& the rows of metal trailers
these citizens have bought
to die in

I will not be found sleeping
at the final toll of bells
or guns
in such a place of waste

The point of departure
is the fire, is that new pleasures
young apricots, return
of the bees
must turn the sylvan back
from leisured sleep, from
hesitation & accumulated capital

What occurs here is the ultimate sorrow
of mere development, is consumption
without accretion
of thought
              inattention to material—
arborite & plywood & these
ornamental cedars are like our lives
they lack *virtu* they simply
tire out with age & turn to junk, have
to be discarded.
              Like the objects
we produce & our homes
our lives are produced, carried out
to be deservedly thrown away
in some space illsuited for anything more useful.

I can see the Form
the rows of trailerpads & tacky
recreation halls exhibit
I'm saying the market
must take its place in eternity
& the ultimate questions
of paradise & the fire

without poetic sentiment & epitaph

The problem is one of how to enclose in the poem the idea & truth that what has wreaked this condition on this civilization is the notion that work is separate from serious knowledge & pleasure. What is so frustrating is that one is confronted by *stupid work* & the parallel idea that freedom consists of the right not to work. What is clear is that the economic system we live under has deliberately institutionalized this construct as a means of perpetuating itself despite the fact that what makes humans unique & interesting, even, I would think, from a point outside the species, is not our pleasures but the tie between intelligence & work that has marked all our advances. We do not, should not, seek pleasure / leisure as the processional stimulus nor as final goal.

The Death of Robin Hood   *a bedtime story for my son*

He is asleep
when we find him, a fly
drinks from the corner of his eye
his white hair is matted & dirty. The light

candle bright in the cellar
at the back of the abbey & at the gate
the oaks drop leaves of gold
in the rain, a cat
stirs in the woodpile

                    John dead
Richard dead
to no avail, the cream
white maggots drop from his guts
onto his great sword
laid out & tarnished by the years

So many. The forest, the few men
in green, the bow, the hooves
of pursuing horses
                    the simple pleasures
of the glen, the clear streams, trout
the faces of the people
                    & the woman
Marion Fitzwater, buried
near Edwinstowe
away from the soldiers.
                    Only the dead
are not taxed, John said as they lowered
her body into the earth, hers & the others,
the Friar who married them
                    not the bad food
but November rain, bad lungs,
too many years.

                    Footfalls
of soldiers outside, this life
despite Richard, the brief years
worthless.

Robin Hood sleeps, turning
bedsores on the straw. Dreams
agonies of forest, woodcutters, many
soldiers steelhelmuted, spears. So
he turns, alarming the fly, & the fly

comes to rest again.
                    The church, these
men and women in black,
                              their prayers
like the lowing of cattle
                              & it is come
to this, sick & alone.

The woman, this one a cousin, bitter
at the lost lands, the new king's bounty,
takes vespers,
                 takes a knife
to the old man's cellar bed
                              & against
his arm gently she lays, & deftly
across
        the blood spurting up
gorgeously red

                        Saint George in this hour
                        of death bring no more soldiers
                        but white maggots
                        for my sorrow, dragons
                        for the morrow. . .

Creatures of State

When I was ten, I played marbles with a boy named Clifford Gibbs, who lived in a small house on the highway to Giscome, no running water in the house, six or seven brothers & sisters. I didn't play marbles with Clifford Gibbs. I took marbles from Clifford Gibbs who wasn't really good enough to play against me but did, each day losing the marbles he bought with money he could not have had. I put the marbles in the gold & purple sack I kept tied around my belt & went home. Clifford went home on the school bus, I remember his sandy-coloured hair & freckled face thru the windows of the bus as it pulled away in the wintery half-dark.

One saturday afternoon Clifford Gibbs went over the side of the Fraser bridge in the old pickup truck he was riding in with his father & both of them were killed. I watched it later, the darkgreen pickup nosing thru the railing & dropping thru the air. It landed upside down on the dry riverbed & Clifford Gibbs died of a fractured skull. He was lying on his back on his father's body inside the cab of the truck when the rescuers got to the truck. He had a ragged haircut which he got when his father placed a bowl over his head & cut off any hair he could see with a pair of mechanical clippers. There were little patches of hair or dirt on his bare scalp that made him look as if he had mange & he wore suspenders & had the smell people carry when they dont, or cant, take baths.

I remember seeing a movie in which an old man kept his money in a little pouch until some men came to his door. They took the money & for no reason I could understand they punched & kicked him & later there was a golden dog sniffing his hand but the old man was dead. On the path I walked on the way to school lived another old man who so resembled the old man in the movie that I knew that both the golden dog & men who would kill him must also exist. I lived in terror of the day he would open his door to those men.

I am caught in the construction of the Real, in the moment that I wept, or did not weep, for the death of Clifford Gibbs. The moment of what did I do, & not do, the truck about to go thru the railing, the tierod under the cab wobbling & then snapping, the old man about to open his doors to the killers.

As a child I believed that reality was a physical substructure & was therefore always vaguely aware of the system of waterpipes & sewers that lay under & connected the city. So that when the battered pickup went thru the bridge railing or the old man opened his door, there was a failure of the Real, the sewers backed up & gushed out.

37

Later I learned that part of the structure is the images of terror & shame in our lives that do not go away & that have an ability to paralyze us or to turn us to action. That I did not lack such images but rather a consistent ability or courage to turn my face to such things. Turn my face to such things. Turn my face to such things.

No summer's left in the leaves
yellow daisy
dandelion
done.

What's left of the year
isn't fun, one

dry yellow leaf dancing
dying in the sun

Dreaming white roses
in the smoke of morning
furled against the cold
real or imagined. I have
come back to the images
love begins with. Look.

They stand among many
they are empty, pure

they feed no one

Love,
these white petals blowing in the streets
don't retell autumn & winter
not snow, they don't say
we go, watch us go, everything
ends, is in vain.

I said that & I hear you
say it & I
will never say it again

Dull day, & from its shadows
a woman's unsuccessful suicide.

Knife in the womb, several hundred pills
for the pain, & a note on the door for the children
to go to the house of a friend. Someone
came in & saved her life
but not her, *she*
is gone, shadows.

Months earlier she stopped her car on a bridge
but a stranger stopped her
he thinking a mechanical problem, can I
help. Are you

injured, a lady asks me. Can
you see it, can you see this new love
on the rebound. On the rebound
or recoil from the edge of
whatever our lives fall into
without love. Oh

I replied, the uselessness
of shadows, oh

thank you
thank you

If the Will breaks
the world's body counts the hours

until we return, there is
no cheating either what is

or is remembered as existing
nothing protects us from the Real

that pain is clear is, finally
the clarity love demands.

But unanchored by Will we drift
thru the trees & buildings & bodies

lost to the shape halfformed at the heart
of things no one makes up

or escapes the pain of not having.
Outside the mind's intransigence

each complexity of the human
a knot of world muscle.

Or as if there was love at the heart of the world
& a world-heart at the boundaries of love

& the halfformed shapes beyond aloneness, pain
could invade it

to hold us

The Butterfly

is the mind is the flight
of the mind from the weight
of desire. The weight
of desire is the mind's fear
it will crush the Beloved.
The world is the mass of thought
the passion for thought is the self
lies against the breasts of the Beloved
propped up on its elbows, thinks
of letting go, the weight, down
into the Beloved.
                    I love you
I can't. I want you.
The weight of the mind's desire
alights on your shoulder

the world.

I'm caught, meaning that
what is passive
is passive
          & what is duplicitous
allows for movement
in any direction.

Lassie come home. Coded messages
commercials on tv
reading the want ads, looking for

signs of Invisibility. A dog
licking the hand of a dead man. A truck
on the dry riverbed, upside down
a child's hand on my wrist as I write.

The reason the truck didn't explode on impact was

the gastank was empty. But sometimes
there are no reasons invisible

just fire
to consume us.

The Death of Romance

A beat-up truck
dropping thru the air over a dry riverbed

no grace of The Swan
but Time's Wingèd Chariot hurrying near

if I sit watching on the grassy bank.

The river offers neither forgetfulness
in this hell nor the luxuries of liberal sorrow.

The broken bodies in the cab
are planetary in numbers

Love's Argument

All that is left of the Old City
is the love poems thru which
abstractly we cross to the Other
because we can't cross with our hearts.

Our hearts become organs of sense
we enclose with our words
& then strap to our legs to enable
a fast draw. Gunfight

at the O.K. Corrall
despite lyrical protestations & postures

a description of political reality
we are too proud or stupid
to confess & the modes
modes of human separation
are lovelorn & loveworn
by the Old City echoing

I love you do you
love me & no one

knows the shape of
the new city or the new kind of love
we have to have.

I think of the tree
turned white by the full moon
in the next yard, despite
the property was cluttered by the refuse
of low-grade industrial activity.

Shards of concrete from an excavation hole
were likewise disclosed.

In an economic system grounded upon exploitation & energized
    by expansion
the breakdown of common vocabulary is inevitable.

The Theology of Capitalism resides in this breakdown which
    puts irresistable stress on syntax
which defines both the nature & possibilities of the society.

Democratic forms of polity within a modern state depend on
    common vocabularies understood by all to nourish the
    body politic, the people otherwise
are starved for meaning.

Contemporary industrial capitalism exploits this principal by
    destroying the commonality of language & creating within
    the wreckage mystical technical vocabularies (Fortran)
that in passing thru vernacular render it opaque.
The parallel encouragement of totalizing mysticisms within the
    body politic produces further opaqueness & incoherence
    within social syntax. We are starved
for meaning.

Those who will not join the struggle for control over the tools
    of meaning pass alms to the priests of capital who grow fat
on our divine substance.

Fragments of Spring   *for Daphne Marlatt*

Each of us loves.
All of us old enough to know
the craft of that. These coastal blossoms
different from those, visibly spreading
into the interior
because the world repeats itself even if
we can't   & it is Spring.
Each of us at the coast
of desire & the once simple ability to love
is entangled somewhere
inside, a complex of history
new beginnings & endings
that don't make sense
because we live without prophets
& without cities to guide us, those things
gone, victims of what Hesiod called
The War of the Sheep of Oedipus

ii

Beware of flight from the coming
of the new City. We have to learn to desire
the city like we desire that lover
who transforms all that is not
into blossoms. The lover who is leaf & branch
of all you are or do
or else there is a thicket
where you will find the bull-headed one
you can neither appease
nor escape. Sunlit field,
white cows, the truth moving upon it.
The truth is
that these cities resemble our lives.
In the thick of them
carry string. Carry pencil & paper. Carry
pencil paper & string in case of emergency.
While entangled in a thicket
regard the shiny leaves you imagine are there
with suspicion, circumspection, with desire.
Write down what you see.

iii

White blossoms spread up the valleys
& the light meets Desire in the still trees.
In the whiteness about your head
learn to know if the shaking is the cold
or the trembling of your desire.
Can you distinguish these blossoms
from the snow.
Do you know your name in Crete
do you know what stood so white
& speechless beneath the trees
do you know what revenge the truth will take
on those who imagine they are free.

iv

We all love
& we find the images of desire
increasingly in the world. Yet
with each valley & canyon
as we travel deeper into the interior
the blossoms grow smaller & less showy.
Sweet whiteness of saskatoon by the roadsides, sage
& finally nothing is visible but
the events of transformation we can't even see.

Organized fragments of a new city
barely visible in the thickets
of desire.

The Hanged Man

gets his feet planted firmly
in the sky

& hangs there
genetalia of the Angelic

leaf & branch, & head
rooted in earth
spreading & securing.
The mind must stay attached

& pulling earth when
the feet move off

in the company of angels.

Stolen Moments

It's always spring
in Paris, black taxis
split for the Louvre
or unload suicides by the Quais,
yellowgreen buds
are endless & useless, promises
blossom unbelieved in
or if,
for a purpose apart
from the city, keeping
the public places barren
because of the vases of spring flowers
left on the table by strangers.

Nothing stolen is really worth having,
nothing manufactured is ever made properly
nothing manufactured can turn the dark wheels
of our hearts
to the newness
I demand for our eyes.

Going into you, that
is my death
   & death to you
if you grow into me.

But I care for you,
your slim bare arms
so naked on the street
in the cold rain. How

could I tell you that?
      Shout
from the windows of my mother's
great house, love,
don't come in here, I
have to come out.

They Used to Say

Night airs are stormy, sweet
with the scent of wild roses, the sea
crashes onto the rocks
beyond the thicket

I have come to my senses.
I've got high-pilèd charactery
on an arborite table, the light
I work by draws moths
& carpenter ants & when I go out

the world seems as exposed
as I am. It will storm
& flower
despite the immanent emptiness
of my life. As if

the modes of polity between human beings
are a chill immanent
in the storm. Our time
is neither good nor easy. How
do I love thee then, how
will I endure the cold how

will I escape the merely personal pathos
of sagging bodies & hearts upheld
by liberal sorrow that the wind doth blow.
Neither complexity nor accuracy
of feeling
will sustain us
& those steel-blue chevies
in the alley
drawn by the sugar of surplus
do not nurture us any more than
a lonely heart pounding
will still the real storm of what is beyond
the personal.
            They never used to say
these inner sweetnesses pushed into everything
became acid but they used to say

we are bereft & I do too

of the world that consumes us,
upholds us in the wind & cold.

Landscape: South of Lilooet

White blossoms of
saskatoon
            & yellow green weeping
willows by the small painted homes
(& shacks for the indians—such things alone

are the substance of love: Human
Commerce & the Transport
of Souls.

Gabriola Island I:

Swift Inspiration;
stink of pulp mill, new moon
some stars, aircraft blinking thru heaven.

Earlier the groceries cost $65
& the supermarket seemed filled
with grotesquely fat people
one woman yelled at my son
''Get out of the way!''
thinking he was her own thinking
children oughta get out of her way. And he

unquiet, unable to handle the silence,
wanting to play games of war
anxious over the absense of telephones, running
water; ancient fears of the dark.

& the sea at night
is beautiful, restless, everything
I already knew it was. It's not
Mother Nature interests me
but the possibility
of human beings bearing down
in the darkness.

Summer Solstice

Purple clouds at the horizon
laced with lavender the trees
blackened by the dusk the wind & sea
a dull roar.
           The precision
of what I see doesn't compensate
for the precision of what is there to see.
they don't match up—like the hummingbird
I saw buzzing angrily
amongst the goldfinches this afternoon
there is a residue of frustration
& cruelty—the bumblebee I smashed
from the air thinking it a whitefaced hornet—
it thought my shirt
was a flower. Thus eventually
nuclear stalemate between the superpowers
derived from the concept of property
to mediate between poor perceptual reflexes
& the world. My neighbour
plants a red flag at the corner of his property
to make sure I can see
where these long weedy grasses end
& his mown lawn begins.

But the light, I have to remind myself
is not merely an aid to perception
which plus technical & social extensions of property
we've come to think of
as Intelligence—Light

has it's own pleasures & I. . .
well, I took the bee from the grass
put it under the rosebush
the dark taught me
to see

Gabriola Island II

High summer, & the air
is full of flying ants : Nature
disposing of its exstatic billions
causing confusion for the working poor
& those few of us fortunate enough
to be sitting on our asses watching ;
woodbugs, the carpenter ants
& me.

I say to my son
High Summer, the stars
in their billions & an abundance
of light.
& these large ants come into it briefly
to find love
& return to the earth.

At first they are winged, but these
torn off by the fucking they mill about
looking for reasons
in the grass, across rocks, falling
into the sea
              without sense
& no place to go, Alas
the brief day
etc.
      but at night
the house is full of them
drawn by the lights.

Avoid them, I tell him
but don't kill them. But
at 2 a.m. trying to read
I get freaked, one's on my neck
& another just shaken from the book
& by 4 hundreds are dead
on the floor

The Four Hills: Sacred Geography   *for Brett Enemark*

The Four Hills that provide perspective
to the life of
the City of
Prince George are:
Connaught, Carney, Cranbrook
& the Cutbanks.

On the first is a park, on the second
a water reservoir on the third
are subdivisions

& on the fourth & last which
is only half there because the river
& hence the name
is an abandoned drive-in cafe used to be called
Look-out Drive-Inn used to look out
over the planer mills on the river flats.
They're gone too. Whispering
only & no guilty sex please, these

are Sacred Places completely untouched
by aboriginal ritual interest
or the serious attention
of the rich
& the poor.

Sacred Geography II

There are three elements:
I am the first
pushing two ways,
now to the angelic now
to the political where the angelic
is taught. I
was not told to push,
the City is not as it should be
when I drive into it
along 1st Avenue & turn up Victoria
the fine building is gone
my father tore down to enlarge his factory
but Prince George otherwise has been reconstructed
as it was in 1955
the year my father made $110,000 profit. I
looked for the books where I found it
age 14, 1958 not understanding how he then
went on to say
you make money with other people's money
taking the profit & reinvesting it
with money the bank matches so that
your wealth is measured by earning power
& the amount you can borrow. 1955
was a good year, he said
the houses along 2nd Avenue became
a concrete facade. I dreamed that the city
had been reconstructed
as it was, I wept
at its beauty. But the reconstruction
is false, the streets as I walk them
1955, Spring, don't exist
& the old Ukrainian from the house
on 2nd Avenue is a doppelganger.

I go further into it, to 3rd Avenue
where I find the Northern Hardware
gutted by fire
Dan Palumbo is standing in front of his store
cigar tilted upwards in the corner of his mouth
& his wonky eye can shoot ducks same time

he's slipping yr tenspot into the till. Until
I push in the proper direction
local color & selfaction only
is possible. Angels of politics should wrestle
the doppelgangers in the streets
before my eyes. I have introduced
so many elements the streets begin to buckle
under the weight of the Self. A maximum
of four feet of frost during the winters
make it necessary to pave streets
having clay-gravel bases every three years.
Frost boils. & in the soft depressions
the fakes & the angels are crushed
by the heavy trucks hauling
for new construction. Three
elements. I
am the first.
Political angels, shiny & new
wrestle sheer construction for second
& doppelgangers battle substance
for the third & the form
of the City, sad as it seems
is the action of the three.

Gabriola Island III

Trying my heart
against the wheel of the City
the Grey-eyed Lady gone
cynical, unmoved, unmoving

In the dark I begin to push, looking
for the evening star
turns out a jetliner blinking
red, green, white, nothing

but the cloud obscuring
all movement but the spreading
racket & filth of the motors
churning the darkness we are

lost in

Lover's Quarrel

I can't sleep
& now there are cop cars
across the street red lights
spinning in the turrets
& the crackle of radio, one cop
talks to another in the next car.
It's a lover's quarrel

& I huddle naked by the window
knowing they aren't looking for me, why
would they look for me what
are they talking about out there
anyhow.
          Well, the rich
sleep on in peace
having given some small tax to the poor
& to the poets
who give in return their words & dreams
& eventually their asses
without being asked.

These days the cops don't even break down the door
looking for what poets have got to say. Eventually

sleepless lovers, poets & politicos
will riot in the streets because of it. Eventually
all of us. Awakened
from sleep. As if

in this nakedness
the first doors are smashed open
disturbing the uneasy sleep of poetry, opening
the quarrel of

what must be said
& what must be

Coming up into it, it also was darkness
in which he was suddenly tired, tired

of Poetry's feathery network rescuing signals
from the obscurity of what we intend turned by

the pressure of events wanting to free
the rider or agent
                    which is the cold
in the moonlight.

So that in the moonlight
wondering whether she could see

he turned around

Crowds laugh at death & pain
in the movies, slurp rootbeer
put their smelly shoes on the backs of our necks.
They also
will die.
        But there really is a dying swan
lost in this world even if
the white flowers have come
merely to obscure the red.

Hookers on Davie Street shoot junk
to ease their senses
muscle cars grind metal against metal

& at the horizon a yellow moon rising
calls forth this harvest

of our indifference

Is it enough that Angels
fuck with mortals
in the backs of those customized
flamepainted panel trucks can

we make a revolution of that
put an end to exploitation
by throwing open the back doors
for everyone to see that the form
of the Invisible
is just like you & me Yes

it is a girl it is
an Angel how
will it distribute equitably
the wealth of nations

"The Celestial Grid of Language is gone."
so the Beauty of God
replaces the beauty of His Power

because we have stepped on His Cord
pulling him forward into
the Visible World.

This subsumes the fact
someone told me he died in 1900
apparently of a broken heart

but the truth is His Thought
is now dangerous

Today I learned about Dialectical Materialism
& the Class Struggle
in which I've been engaged most of my adult life.

but my longstanding relation
to the White Goddess & the Muse of Bullshit
makes me use the words I learn
distrustfully, almost timorous
of their historical pedigree
& the emotional charge set off by their use.

Which I'm convinced isn't any different
than those adds on T.V. for toilet paper
or orange juice from Florida. I'd like
to commit Dialectical Materialism & Anita Bryant
to the Hell's Angels for two weeks
to see if they come out less charged
with that certainty that is abuse
to the mind & its astonishments
in the world.

Looking at the moon
on a motorcycle at 70 mph
should put both in the ditch
where the poets
are supposed to be at work

Language is the first political energy:
The first problem
is conjunctive, *conjunction*
the joining together of two elements
delights us.

The problem arises from the expulsion by the two
of all Others, the resulting order
oppressive. *The Police, in conjunction with
the Army, established order.* And the people
correctly want to attack the material connection
& the order
not recognizing the origin of oppression
resides in the substance of
Euro-american syntax & the yoking together
for the sake of order
Necessity & Industrial Labour
thus creating Surplus Value & Capital
as the allies of Order.

Hurry up, it's getting late is the energy
of the Substantial, also *an arranging
in order for battle* besides, alongside
beyond, behind, above
without conventional connectives
altering the substance of how things get done
what the people are to attack
what is to be ordered.

At first no one will understand
this suddenly vertical arrangement of material—
daffodils line up with diesel buses
the soldiers, police
lost in the crowd
of new, familiar relations & clouds
disperse in all directions
as if panicked

by the moonlight

The house at midnight
half-lit, one by one
turning out the lights, the dog
still outside the door
won't go home, the tide
falling back in the quiet

Demanding to know
what the intentions of thought
are, the voices echoing in the dark
are ghostly, are
talking about cars. Drunks
on sunday night. As if the moonlight
gave up on us & drank all the love
from the world when we landed
only ourselves on the moon.

Despite the astronauts, it
(the love, moonlight
when it falls around me now
is still more silvery than astronauts.

And because of it,
hollow voices, the dog
doesn't even bark
at the drunks.

A branch of flowering cherry for you
lady
cut from a public tree, small, roughbarked
to the touch
& the rough skin on your arms, pointed breasts
beneath the folds of your dress
lovely to the touch

despite these boring suburbs
& the physical distance between human lives.
There is poplar, birch, fir
thickets of red alder between the old & new
& already rundown houses.

I brought these branches & left them by your door
because you weren't home

By your gate were golden forsythia, the sun
breaking open the weeping willows, lady

lady inside the pale pink blossoms
the year is stirring
the breeze is warm
& coils around the slender boughs

& ankles of

Gravel
& Maillardville. The church
in the rain. The Virgin
in concrete & the mandala
is colourless
because her thousand lovers
are poor.
            I have lost my heart
watching the rain
fail to wash the flyash from her body.
Our cheeks are wet from this world's
tears & sorrows

but the city rushes on & past
heartlessly

What is possible to say, what does anyone
need to hear

concerning trees along the public streets public
aesthetics blowing in the near-hurricane force of the wind

of public & personal change.
                         There must be places
for the sparrows that huddle in the rain
contained in these momentous public changes.

Or else this shivering will never cease
at the doorways of the Possible
& the poor & the lovers will be indistinguishable
against the solid facade

of the city streets

Not supposed to be writing any longer about
loving, rather
the endless common difficulty
of finding suitable partners
for crimes against the state we are in.

These criminal
blossoms on the table, blooming
despite you are gone.

The forms of love are a constant puzzle
not the least the puzzle of
should love exist at all.

How can such things exist
while the streets are filled
with the poor & with lovers all

tired & hungry

Waking up to your tears
2 A.M. my cock halfhard
against your back
the hamster in the kitchen
running its wheel, what

am I
to do, I'm entangled
in love, your tears falling
across my arm trapped under you
cradles your head and it's years
beyond the ancient dream of romance & light;
That's gone
like the ordered world I knew as a child
& the justice I expected was it's source.

Tonight I only want to know
what did I do, do I deserve this,
lying in the depths of love
tracing routes down
into the tears I awoke to
my cock halfhard against your back
the squeaking wheel the hamster turns
into the traffic
of personal misery.

is this the city, is this night flower
the real world is love tangled past hope.
My hand is half open
half fist   in a dark
no longer unborn light. What

is the hamster   where
is the child   Why
in this wakening

is it you
that I fight

keep talking. There
is the Terror of love
that it grows
from the words it feeds
to the leopards of desire.

My mouth against your breasts
begin love's death
choking the words
the leopards desire

II

After Dante

the second life proceeds
unlike the first
tense & vigilant
against stupid bullshit
& descriptive nature. Love

your nature is
particular, mixt with
the new events
& barely invisible

III

After Dante

is it language itself
stops up my mouth
or the warriors of Will
hunting the streets for leopards

because no words can speak
when everyone is free & everyone
is alone amongst leopards. Can I

ever speak directly of Love's pure body
in the absense of that vast yellow flower
of an impossibly organized world.

After Dante the streets
are the same
but I have stopped
at the intersections
where words still touch things
& each goes off alone
dirtydancing in the dark which is
beyond desire & the silence
where angels are

IV

After Dante

I am not the same.
Watching you sleep 2 a.m.
March snowy night. If only
there was nothing else to say

i.e. Kenneth Patchen's misery
not the result of privilege & abuse
of human labour & he

not also given up to
blind increase

V

After Dante

the sun again eventually gleams
on the blue sea, those pretty white patches
on the distant mountains
really are snow

& a lonely heart is none of these.

A white boat (you can see the multiple lines
tempting the dark fishy water

edges past the shimmering point
& into the calmer waters

The poetics of cities

must change, can
no longer be based on material resource alone
or absolute planetary wealth   the earth
is finite & mortal
hence the need for new poetics
of diminution.
                    I want to say
I love you to someone
or simply walk the streets with friends
but the poetics of this are trapped
in the enterprises of liberation
& in the complexity of it's technology
most of all in the minds
of those who build & rule the cities:
moneymen, planners, the elect, hence

the streets are hostile, abundance
fears its sheer mass.

The overpopulated human species is the source
of new wealth
the social the form
of the poetics

We do require meaning to subsist & we do demand
in however small a context to know
what's going on, what's our place
& who are these men in uniform do
they protect us, & what further, beyond
questions of property & personal gain what
will make strangers desire our company
& our bodies. This

is permission for the use of
the plural, is the real struggle going on, this

& a wondering heart (angel wings
I saw on the beach turned out
iridescent seaweed
                          is the Angelic

& the gorgeous wings brush us
when we stand in the darkening waters
of all that it is not

& we are part of

The Mystery of Love fades,
takes off the belt, buckler,
the corset of gold. Real women
often wear coloured underwear
bought at the Bay.
Let them.
Paradise is not artificial, isn't elegant
& nakedness
no longer reveals us an angels
nor does it betray
the pain in each of our hearts. I demand

a great love without wings.
With real roads, bridges, the records of our human deeds
piling up on the city register.
                              & in the seat of Power
a compassion capable of boredom, anger
curiousity & finally action
worthy of the tangle
of flesh, trees, metal, the landscape

we are
together in

By Reason of the Beautiful
I search these streets to find her
but not from the illusions caused by
the illusion of the perfectly parallel.
The streets fascinate, this solitude
is a torture. The city is invisible
& this heart wholly visible
because I have come to question the Reason
of the Beautiful. Yet

you, Beloved, I do not question, do
love & do
not love finally.

I will never find her.

May 15, 1975

Spotted cows in green fields
the valley not of the heart
but of the stomach.
                    Green shoots of corn
& grass, birds, lombardy poplars, barns
bridges, silos, kids
hitchhiking to Hope.

I hope they get there
I hope these fields bear crops
the spotted cows give milk
the clouds beyond the hills bring rain.

Survival of the body is a necessity
even the blackbirds must eat
but the radio says *Better Value*
will deliver all over the valley

& it's time to stop believing it.
Each year more land falls fallow
bought up by speculators
& the silos fall to subdivision.

In the nearest field a pink trailer
still on blocks blocks the view
(in Cuba 30 acres is the most one man can own
& the least he can till)
but here each 10 acres is parcelled
with no increase in taxes when the land isn't used—
The fundamental questions of food & shelter
are unanswered
& the opportunists & the ignorant flock in
to profit in the silence.

Rail tracks run beside the freeway
Portuguese dangle white legs
from white boxcars, spotted cows
the clouds, fields
riddled with rootmaggots
redwinged blackbirds eat redwinged blackbirds

killed by the speeding trucks

yellowgreen willows, maples, silvergreen poplars
in the draws   each year
the things we live with

more distant
more tenuous

The Address of the Watchman

The economies of coming home
under the wheels of the car
become facts of life :
                    Black pavement
Williams Lake at dusk, McLeese Lake
Quesnel, Hixon, Stoner
the road stretching into the starless dark etc.
eventually the lights of the city, Prince George

Too many things said & done without enough accuracy
too much careless speech & most of my life
a waste of precious time. I can't go back
over the errors to get them right
just like the errors a city makes
are too costly to rectify. So I go on
watching & waiting, knowing the question

is *what's here* & what can we do
in the face of what we know isn't here.
Who built this house
& to whom after all fires
will it belong. Paradise
is the end of the world as we know it
the ancient stories are confused now, the signal fires
are visible from all directions
& the ox is gone from my tongue.

So I want to speak at length of what I've seen
& see, Troy in ruins 3000 years
& in this place
people live & die without understanding
either the fires stretched along the horizon
or their lives.
                    & Paradise
is the end of the world as we know it

Tabor Mountain Poem

Today the air is clear
I can see the absense of
the death of

useable timber. Today

the Grove & Tsus fires
are thickets of willow & douglas maple, thistles
dandelions & some half-assed replanting
by the government.

Tabor Mountain burned off August 1961 mostly in one night
65 mph winds blew up two small fires into 50,000 acres
& the destruction my life has become entangled in
the recourse of. Yes of course

this is personal, learning that human beings
are to be viewed askance
& at some slight distance if possible
24 hours a day

which is too hard:
Most of the men on the firelines
slept 14 hours a day
not fighting the fire
nor the system of human relations that brings them
to goof off in the face of
both a very personal & visible danger
& the destruction of vast numbers of living things.

Some of the better off equipment owners
abandoned old cats to the fire
to be replaced by new machines
at public expense

but the poor merely bickered & bitched
at the lousy food & services given them
in exchange for desultory labour
not interested in saving a landscape
they knew would later be destroyed

for somebody else's profit

& there was one young kid busted for bringing beer
into the firecamps
& another, older & a cook, was stealing food
from the kitchens, fingered him.

I was 17 years old, stood watching
a pillar of smoke lowering in the sky.

I can see what we did here
I can see what we're doing

Second Tabor Mountain Poem

We expect desolation
of everything, I expect this desolation here
seeded by the limits of contemporary imagination

now visible from Tabor Mountain
& anywhere.
            But this is a child's constructed landscape
overgrown with the paraphanalia & debris
of a system of human activity that simplifies
both nature & human life
in order to exploit it.

Children grow rough or bitter against it
given neither difficulty nor splendour, given
these ashes & broken trees
no phoenix will rise from, maybe

human beings can rise from them, as do
the dandelions & thickets of maple & willow, eventually
some carefully tended trees
that will stand long after

I will be ashes

Third Tabor Mountain Poem

Fire burns. That's
the law. usually associated
with messing around with something
or someone you don't understand
& someone else doesn't want you to understand.

But now poetry concerns the light
on these burned-over hillsides. & aside from
an unimportant personal allegory
the kind of light I'm looking for
forces me to declare war
on the fire. At some point obscured by smoke
I can't see thru & am losing interest in
I foresee nothing but ashes.

William Carlos Williams goodbye.

All them featherless chickens in that shed
over there beside the conveyor belt
don't agree with what poetry has come to mean

& them thinshelled watery eggs
for consumption by lovers
of what is rare & almost certainly sterile
goodbye to you too.

It isn't enough to burn the chicken coop
for heat to warm our cold cold hearts.

Light. And those of us who stay inside
where hearts are finally hardboiled

don't matter

Prince George, August 8, 1976

Goat Island is disappearing from under the bridge
where someone once presumably kept goats
& in the 1940's kids built a ropeladder to get to the island
lost their shoes, some fell, some got drunk & drowned
blah blah

another boring story
no one knows the truth of
except that the island is still there
& one can watch the river in the rain
as I do, & smell the pulp mills, watch the riverboats
dock beneath the bridge.
                              Meaning that
there *is* a story here, a totality
of internal & external events
that brings me to these tears rolling down my cheeks
because I've come back here without interest
in what is sentimental or personal history
& there is a city despite all attempts to deny it.

Goat Island will be gone one day
following the goats that may never have been there.
& I'm no different.

But Old Man River & the trucks
rolling east/west on the bridge
stay on like Truth, Terror

& a delight at being human
which is a return

from exile

For Barry McKinnon

There's an old man walking the sidewalk
was a young man once, & not so old either
when I was a child he chased me two blocks
after I broke his window. Accidentally
of course. Of course he grew old

Joy says, now he gets drunk every day
cause the old bitch broke his heart. Related to
the McKinnons who no longer live here
& the Masseys, Roger who married Lois or Mavis
who married a busdriver, also a drunk.

And the youngest daughter, Kathy, was my first love,
married an english sailor. What could I say.
Railroad people, all of them. They come
& they go. Like my father, trying to grow fruit trees
in this northern cold for 25 years. Tiny plums
without any sugar & sour crabapples. & we

are left to follow such men
or to rectify their errors.

Well Barry we don't walk down to the Prince George Hotel
every morning for a beer
but we do get there eventually
2 A.M. on my last night in town.
& we don't get as drunk as they did
& still do. Plums & crabapples in the cold summer rain
offer a possibility of
a little sweetness.

There's an old man walking the sidewalk
was a young man once.

So

I go on by the ashdark lake
these few years of my life
observing the rebirth of
this fire-ravaged landscape, observing
the blackbirds eat the dead fish, & yeah

the vast black wings of my Angel do sometimes
lift me where poets are trained to go

but there is no grace in it
there is no grace.

I come back to watch Clifford Gibbs falling
end over end inside the dark green truck, again
& again I watch the back wheels spin aimlessly
in the failing light.

My own wheels spit gravel & dust
as the car digs up the mountain road
into the Grove Burn, August 1976

We are not given grace
we are given these burned-off hills

whatever our yearnings
we must learn how to face

August 22, 1976

The green fields are not of the mind
not of the stomach
& not of the heart. They are green fields
pocked with late dandelions, buttercups
even daisies, & unploughed. These things

are not the sky, nor are they our lives
except in the shadow
because our lives are without density
& divorced from their consequences.

We accept poor merchandise for value
& a choice between what is so near
it is obscure
& a landscape so distant
our bodies don't know it's pleasant breezes
or seek shelter from its storms.
                                    The smoke
signals us from the distant mountains
& the roar of trucks (115 decibels)
to those nearnesses

at the touch of a hand, beside us & loving
we can't hear our own voices to speak

the sense of.

The *Substantial* is the grace, is not
Materiel
nor is it *Spirit*
               but rather the difficulty
of staying in an informed heart
Letting loose the hunger that is there
for substance   to be informed also by
the *Otherness* of things, which likewise
is not *Materiel* nor is it
Spirit.

It asks me to ride
a black horse & a white horse,
so here I sit tall in the saddles looking hard
at the distances, hat tipped back
like Gene Autry
               these *Blue Canadian Rockies*

I could sing
but the song is caked with
electronic technology & an american vision
via Billy Graham & the parasequent divisions
into binary functions, labours

losing both horses

& by which (since abt 1900) we can
sing our songs
but not in the streets
with all men & women

so that the songs we know
& those we hear
are not the issue.
               For the personal
there is the search for horses

& beyond it great difficulty:
The *Substantial*, the World.

*Such that the song is heard
amongst our children.*

Noon News

reports a lone gunman on 3rd floor
4th & Fir, Vancouver
clear winter day, the air so clean
you can't taste it
              The radio reports
from across the street & brought to us
by Money's Mushrooms sez the announcer
What Food These Morsels be
                            while the police
move to the second floor, sweating by doorways
with the barrels of highpowered rifles
pressed against to cool their necks the gunman
holds a woman on the 3rd floor
he threatens to kill, she whimpers in fear

so that I'm caught between that image
of a woman about 40, blonde hair
& Shakespeare's dust rustling somewhere

Buses roll on Broadway, the News fades
& eventually all words shake loose
from the entanglement
to sharpen themselves against both time & events:

Eventually one man in critical condition, the woman
dead & the cops push the gunman into the back
of a black car & drive away

the News is brought to us
by Money's Mushrooms yeah

What Food These Mortals be

Point Grey   *for Robin Matthews*

Ten years looking out
at Black Mountain
& southeast Howe Sound / Burrard Inlet
rain & mist

which is what I was supposed to do
at Black Mountain—look into
what is my own.

The CP Ferry in the mist
w/ red triangle on stack
freights goods for industry—
the old confident shit abt industry carrying goods
for industry

but there's no propane on the islands
because the distributor is an ex-MLA hostile
to the socialist government & wont settle with the union

In the mist the clay banks of Point Grey pull down
from lack of silt redirected by the causeway on Iona Island
& the city govt wants to shore up the coast
with a road so the lazy can drive
away the last few humans in the city
go naked when the weather. . .

All of which ignores the question
of the governance of the elements

of Beauty & / or
the inland sewage pouring out of the Fraser
on the south side of the promontory

All of which
is mine

not as property
or even as most poets
now take the Local—
as resource

to be exploited

by which means generally the mist will remain
& the governance of language will remain
in the force of a translucence grows
more oppressive each day if

cargoless ferries ride this crest of sodden light
& our soft words carry us
& our loved ones willingly
to the other side

Silver limousines on Burrard & 4th
white heads, open-mouthed, within
turn from side to side
talking. Shades
for the bright sunlight, black suits
for the mortician, the mourners.

They must be hot in there, nothing on the street
acknowledges this death
the mourners & the dead
stopped by a light
one last intersection
of the journey to the grave. I'm going

the other way, downtown to buy a new pair of pants
& if I try to imagine a whole human life
all the things done & those
undone, I don't believe
the white heads behind the tinted glass
of silver limousines I believe

the honking horns, the limousines
glide across this intersection
to the next, the white-haired
men & women still talking
& looking out the windows

The Stone

Daily the weight of the stone grows
the difficulty of remembering
when I walk the streets I am

walking on the street, people
are starving & my car
has an oil leak. I keep thinking

it's coming, *it's coming*
to this, to me
at me, the weight

on my reluctant shoulders
& in this ancient story
what does he stand on, is it

the glory of the stone, the gravity
of the effort to right
a bad world.
                Sparrows darken the air
love fails, women fail
as men have failed
to be just, the conditions
of our lives won't improve
unless the political & economic forms
that oppress us all

are broken, & yeah
women may lead us to it, even so

the stone is squarely on my
male shoulders, denying me pleasure
I might have to comfort me without misgivings
in this dark—lyric tensions
I know, but sparrows in the body
& the mind is winged
must lead
thru the systems of love & romance
that serve us in the absense
of a goodness we can earn & share

where the stone sits barren & silent
what our lives are
covering over
what might be

Song

What of our lives, our bodies
wasting in misery we can see
no reason for, simple despair
despite the new car parked on the street, the T.V.
on & making dinner in the kitchen.

History crowding against the Personal.
The things that break hearts
also exist in history. But the artists
have forgotten history & the politicos
have forgotten the broken & breaking
hearts. & those of us who know both
or learn that broken hearts mean nothing
unless history mends the world that breaks them
ask of our lives, our bodies wasting
in misery, move than simple despair
we can see complex reasons for

If the city is to be more than merely
a collection of loves
or attempts to love, if
it is not to go the way of most love,
mile upon mile of oily beach
for the ocean to drag into the ocean

& now I see our loves
without profit or loss
of form
         our real needs
do not profit us
                    & the city
as we know it neither starves our bodies
nor fills our hearts

How not to give in to
the magnificence of cities, shining sp
in the morning distance, wet birches
in quiet streets & the traffic
at 6 A.M., lights flickering on
in houses, people moving softly
not to wake
                systems of dismay syster
how never to give in to
while they steal & tear
the force of men & women
for power & gain
                the rain
just falls when I really look
close on

        This awful tension
of living in one kind of world
& imagining another, this city
changed, people coming & going
amongst spires & magnificence
they have sense of, & responsibility
driving their cars or whatever else
is not poetry but might be good

wanting poetry to become more
than a structure of shining dreams
not possible
to give in to
the belief of

November 23, 1976

how to make angels matter
to what we are lost in the midst of

put those feathery monsters to work
in a more useful job than this constant

reorganization or our narcissism. The didactic
is angelic because the black smoke & stench of diesel

is now aether
                    the turning of their blackened wings
must learn to clear
                              the snapping of tierods
under a truck
                    so that the flight of
& the death of
                    broken bodies cushioned by
broken bodies
                    can cease

Discourse

               now in the air
& it confronts us, my fellow

Poets. What we know of common things, e.g.
how this man in his economic relations to others
creates an effect which is felt in heart & stomach
be it he is a nice man & drinks heartily, makes speeches
of good things, loves children
                       this discourse
is the green forest, the wilderness
to which we no longer go alone
nor with fine & frenzied eyes a' rolling.

Said simply, there are so many of us
poets & other mortals, this discourse, how
we will live on this earth among many

is common cause, is the difficulty
denying the pleasure, the now false sociality
of image, metaphor in the isolation
of the mind.
             These tools are taken, misshapen
to render the condition of all most profitable
to a few
        who like us drink heartily, make speeches
of good things, love children
                   & use our tools
better than we, breaking words on them—

Our stiff branches, the curves of body
the sun, the self
        are lovely but
Beauty is the glory of the Good
& the air is ugly with words crowding us

& too many starve, we starve, this discourse

is now the air, is
our lives, my
fellow Poets

Systems of production
have been thoroughly done
Love, Sex, Death
& Economics.

People need work to live
but there is no reason for humiliating them
or for sentimentalizing it. Like sparrows

human beings are hungry.
& will remain so despite systems
of production for Love, Sex, Death
& Economics.

The sparrows outside on the grass
consume all they find
of human waste, substance & seed

My heart will break before it comes
the revolution will not come before
all of it is broken, the revolution
will break all hearts.
                              Let the hearts
of poets & politicos twist & break
for their poor imagination
of what we might have

let them pump into the streets
let us see what we have, this

pattern for subdivision
& progressive alienation
of public lands
                    despite the discourse
of all those white sheets on the clotheslines of the poor
behind Main street
whipping in the polluted breeze.

All our plans will turn red
from the gore of the Personal

& we will lift it, finally
from us

breaking our hearts

Marxist Sparrows, Angels of Fascism, Creatures
of State : The winged creatures fall
from the air, the fog is so thick today
airplanes can't even land, no one can leave
or come home.

We won't find either love or political justice
in this city if each is a sparrow
chittering in the cold.

Our lives are as blurred by the business
of looking out for ourselves as the city is
by the fog. The planes can't land
or take off despite our wonderful instruments
of pleasure. And neither can we.

Angels of Marxism, Fascist sparrows. Such divisions
bear witness to
the cold & the hunger
that divide us in the leafless tree the fog
that hides us & will bring us
inevitably to ground
in cities where angels bear arms

& the sparrows are fed at last.

May 11, 1977
Vancouver